AROHA JOY

MOTAGBA'S RACING HEART

Copyright © 2024 by Aroha Joy

All rights reserved. No part of this publication may be reproduced, stored or transmitted in any form or by any means, electronic, mechanical, photocopying, recording, scanning, or otherwise without written permission from the publisher. It is illegal to copy this book, post it to a website, or distribute it by any other means without permission.

First edition

This book was professionally typeset on Reedsy.
Find out more at reedsy.com

This book is dedicated to God Almighty

Contents

Preface		ii
Acknowledgments		iii
1	The Beginning of a Race	1
2	The Weight of Victory	5
3	Reflections in Silence	10
4	The Crossroads of the Heart	15
5	The Storm and the Calm	20
6	The Unseen Path	25
7	The First Step	30
8	The Unknown Horizon	33
9	The Silent Mentor	37
10	The Return of the Heart	41

Preface

Motagba, once celebrated as the fastest runner in his village, finds himself trapped in a race he never intended to run—the race for approval, recognition, and success. Pressured by the expectations of his family and community, he feels the weight of his own heart beating faster and faster, urging him to achieve more, to be more. But the louder the world around him becomes, the more Motagba realizes he is losing himself in the pursuit of speed and glory.

In search of clarity, he leaves the familiar paths of his village and embarks on a journey into the wilderness, where silence and solitude force him to face the truth about himself. There, he learns that the real race is not one of outward achievement, but an inward journey toward understanding, self-acceptance, and inner peace.

As Motagba returns home, having discovered that the true measure of a person's worth lies not in their speed or accomplishments but in their connection to their roots, family, and community, he brings back a wisdom that not only transforms him but also reshapes the way the village sees success.

Motagba's Racing Heart is a story of self-discovery, of letting go of external pressures and embracing the journey of finding one's purpose. It reminds us that sometimes, the race we are meant to run is not the one we think we are on, but the one that leads us back to where we truly belong.

Acknowledgments

Thank you for your love and support

1

The Beginning of a Race

Motagba's heart pounded wildly as the sun began to dip below the horizon, casting a golden glow over the village of Obadagba. His hands shook with a nervous energy he couldn't shake, his thoughts racing faster than his own pulse. This wasn't just any race—it was *the* race. The one that could change his life forever.

Since he was young, Motagba had always been known as the fastest runner in Obadagba. His speed was the stuff of local legend, a gift he inherited from his father, who had been a champion in his own time. But this race, the annual Obadagba Festival Sprint, was different. This time, it was about more than just winning. It was about proving something deep within himself, something he had only begun to understand in recent weeks.

Motagba had spent months preparing for this race, training in the early hours of the morning before the village awoke. He had run through the hills, across the fields, and along the winding paths that led into the heart of Obadagba. His legs burned with the memory of each grueling step, but it wasn't the physical pain that haunted him. It was the pressure. The expectations. His father had never spoken of it, but Motagba knew the old man's eyes would be watching him from the crowd, judging, waiting.

The path he would race along was familiar—gravel roads, patches of rough terrain, and narrow turns that required precision and speed. The race would be the ultimate test of his strength, speed, and stamina. But as he stood at the starting line, Motagba couldn't shake the nagging feeling that something was missing. It wasn't the race that frightened him—it was the silence in his heart.

He glanced over at the other runners, each one adjusting their shoes or stretching their limbs, but Motagba couldn't bring himself to look too long. His competition was fierce this year. Among them was Ireti, a new contender who had come to Obadagba just a few months ago. She was quick, sharp, and had already beaten some of the older villagers in their informal races. And then there was Olamide, a friend turned rival, who had always been in Motagba's shadow, yet this year seemed more determined than ever to leave it behind.

Motagba's mother, who had always supported him quietly from the sidelines, was there too. She had never understood the full weight of his desire to run, but she had always encouraged him, telling him that his speed was a gift that should be shared with the world.

With a deep breath, Motagba finally looked up at the sky. The sun was nearly gone, and the air had begun to cool, the gentle breeze teasing his sweat-soaked skin. He closed his eyes for a moment, listening to the sounds of the village preparing for the festival. The beating drums, the excited chatter, and the occasional call of a bird soaring above—it all felt so distant, as if the world itself was holding its breath.

"Are you ready?" came the voice of the race marshal, pulling Motagba back to the present. The old man's eyes were sharp, his hands steady, but his voice had a certain weight to it. Motagba nodded, though his throat felt tight, his heart still racing.

The marshal raised his arm, signaling the start. The other runners shifted in place, their muscles taut, their eyes focused on the path ahead.

Then, with a quick motion, the marshal dropped his arm, and the race began.

Motagba took off like a shot, his feet hitting the earth with a rhythmic force that had become second nature. He could hear the others close behind him, but he didn't dare look back. His world had narrowed to the rhythm of his breath, the pounding of his heart, and the beat of his legs as they moved in perfect synchrony. The wind rushed past him, a blur of motion and freedom.

This was what he lived for.

But as the race carried on, something strange began to happen. His heart, which had once felt like a steady drumbeat, began to falter. It wasn't that his body was tired—he was faster than ever, pushing his limits with every step. But his mind, his thoughts, they were beginning to cloud. The faces of those watching, the hopes of his father, the pressure to win—they all seemed to weigh heavier on his chest with each passing second.

Motagba knew something was wrong. His legs were still strong, his breathing steady, but his heart—his heart was racing in a way it had never done before. It was as if something was calling to him, something beyond the finish line, something beyond the village itself.

As the finish line came into view, a sharp pain shot through his chest, and for the briefest moment, Motagba thought he might collapse. But he couldn't stop now. He couldn't fail.

With a final burst of strength, Motagba surged ahead, crossing the finish line in a blur. He didn't look back. He didn't even hear the cheers of the crowd. All he could focus on was the pounding of his heart, as if it were trying to tell him something—something important.

And in that moment, Motagba realized that the race had only just begun.

2

The Weight of Victory

The crowd's roar reverberated in Motagba's ears as he stood still, frozen at the finish line. He could feel his chest heaving with every breath, his heart still racing as though it had never stopped. The world around him seemed to blur into the background, the faces of the cheering villagers blending together, their voices becoming a distant hum. All he could hear was the rapid thudding of his heart, echoing louder with each passing second.

He had won. But why did it feel like a hollow victory?

Motagba's legs trembled beneath him as he took a step forward, trying to move but feeling as though the ground beneath him was shifting. His breath came in quick bursts, his pulse pounding in his temples. He had crossed the finish line first, but the sense of triumph he expected to feel didn't come. Instead, there was only an emptiness—a strange, gnawing feeling in the pit of his stomach.

"You did it!" A voice cut through the fog of his thoughts, and Motagba looked up to see Olamide jogging toward him, a wide grin spread across his face. "You actually did it! I thought for sure I was going to beat you this time."

Motagba managed a smile, but it didn't reach his eyes. Olamide clapped him on the back, his excitement contagious, but Motagba couldn't bring himself to feel the same. He had won, yes, but it felt like there was something more he was meant to discover, something that had eluded him during the race. The heavy feeling in his chest didn't lift, no matter how hard he tried to shake it off.

"Thanks," Motagba muttered, trying to sound enthusiastic. He wanted to be happy. He wanted to celebrate. But the truth was, he couldn't. Not yet.

The crowd around them continued to cheer, some people rushing forward to congratulate him, others shouting in disbelief at how fast he had run. His mother appeared beside him, her face beaming with pride, her arms wide as she enveloped him in a warm embrace.

"You're incredible, my son," she whispered into his ear, her voice filled with affection. "I knew you had it in you. You made us all proud."

Motagba swallowed hard, nodding mechanically. "Thank you, Mama." But even as he said the words, he couldn't shake the feeling that something wasn't quite right. The victory didn't feel as sweet as he had imagined. There was a weight to it, a pressure he couldn't explain.

He looked across the field and saw Ireti standing off to the side, her expression unreadable. The moment their eyes met, she gave him a small nod, a gesture of acknowledgment, but it felt distant, as if there was something unsaid between them. Ireti had been his closest competition, and though he had won, something in her demeanor told him that she was not defeated, not in the way he had expected.

Motagba felt a pang of guilt, as though he had let her down in some way. Ireti was more than just a contender—she had become his friend. She had challenged him in ways no one else ever had, and now, with the race behind them, there was a silence between them that felt heavier than any loss could. He wanted to go over to her, to say something, but he couldn't move. The weight of the moment, the expectations, the pressure, it all felt too much.

His father's face flashed in his mind. He hadn't seen him in the crowd, but he knew the old man would be waiting for him back at home, ready to hear about the race. Ready to hear that his son had lived up to the legacy of his family's speed. But what would he say? Would it be enough? The thought of his father's approval—his unspoken expectations—made his chest tighten even more.

"Motagba!" A voice cut through his swirling thoughts, and he turned to find the village elder, Chief Akintoye, walking toward him with a solemn expression on his face. The chief was an old man, his hair silver and his eyes sharp. Though he was well respected in the village, his face was often stern, his words measured.

"You have done well, my boy," Chief Akintoye said, his voice low but firm. "You have made Obadagba proud today. But there is more to being a champion than crossing the finish line first."

Motagba blinked, surprised by the elder's words. He had expected praise, congratulations, not this cryptic comment. "Thank you, Chief," he said, though his confusion was clear in his voice.

Chief Akintoye's gaze softened, but only slightly. "You are fast, Motagba. No one can deny that. But speed alone will not carry you through life. It is the heart, the spirit, that will determine your true worth. Remember that."

The words hung in the air, weighty and meaningful. Motagba's mind raced, trying to make sense of them. What did the elder mean? Hadn't he just won the race? Wasn't that enough?

Before he could ask, Chief Akintoye turned and walked away, his footsteps steady and purposeful. Motagba watched him go, his thoughts spinning in a dozen directions at once. What did the chief mean by that? What was it about the race, about victory, that he was missing?

"Motagba!" Ireti's voice broke through his thoughts, and he turned to see her walking toward him now, her expression less guarded than before. She gave him a small smile, though it was tinged with something he couldn't place. "Congratulations," she said simply.

"Thanks," Motagba replied, though it felt awkward. "You ran well, too."

Ireti raised an eyebrow. "I did? I thought you had me beat from the start."

Motagba chuckled, but it was forced. "I was lucky."

"Maybe," she said, her tone playful but serious. "But luck doesn't win races. Determination does."

They stood in silence for a moment, neither of them sure of what to say next. The crowd had started to disperse, moving toward the village square where the festival celebrations were taking place. The excitement was palpable, but for Motagba, it felt distant, like something he couldn't quite reach.

"I think I need to go," Ireti said suddenly, her voice soft. "I'll see you later."

Before Motagba could respond, she turned and walked away, her figure blending into the crowd. He watched her go, a strange emptiness settling in his chest once again.

It wasn't just the race. It was everything. The pressure. The expectations. The feeling that he was always trying to live up to something that wasn't even fully clear to him. What did he want? What did it mean to win? What was the point of it all?

His mother's voice broke through his thoughts once more, this time calling him to join her at the village square. He turned and walked toward her, the feeling in his chest growing heavier with every step. The festival was in full swing, and the village was alive with music, dancing, and laughter. But all Motagba could think about was the race, and what lay ahead.

As he joined his mother, she beamed at him with pride. "Come, let's celebrate your victory, my son."

But Motagba's heart wasn't in it. He had won the race, but it felt like the race had only just begun. The true test was not in crossing the finish line. It was in finding peace with the weight of his heart, with the expectations, the pressure, and the knowledge that the path ahead was filled with more than just victory.

And so, Motagba stood amidst the celebration, but his mind was elsewhere, racing toward an unknown future, a future that promised far more than just speed.

The real race had only just begun.

3

Reflections in Silence

The days following the festival passed in a blur. Motagba spent them wandering the village, his mind lost in thought, his heart heavy with unanswered questions. Despite the cheers, the praise, and the warmth of his family and friends, the feeling of emptiness lingered like a shadow that wouldn't lift. The victory was supposed to feel like the culmination of everything he had worked for, but instead, it only brought more uncertainty.

Motagba had spent so much of his life chasing speed, chasing the next race, the next challenge, thinking that winning would be the thing that would finally make him feel whole. But now, he wasn't so sure. What did it all mean? What was the point of running faster than anyone else if it didn't bring peace, if it didn't answer the deeper questions gnawing at him?

The next morning, after another restless night, Motagba woke to the sound of birds calling in the distance, their songs filling the cool morning air. The village was still quiet, the only movement coming from the early risers who were already tending to their fields or preparing for the day's work. Motagba, however, had no particular task to tend to—he had no obligation except to himself, and even that was beginning to feel overwhelming.

His father had been waiting for him at home the night of the festival. He hadn't spoken much, but the proud look in his eyes had said everything Motagba needed to hear. His father's approval, though silent, was always present, like a constant weight on Motagba's shoulders. But now, even his father's pride didn't seem to offer the solace it once had. There was something more, something beyond all of it that Motagba couldn't quite grasp.

He rose from his bed, rubbing his eyes as he stepped outside into the fresh morning air. The village was still sleeping, but Motagba felt the need to move, to clear his mind. The path leading to the hills, the place where he had often trained alone, called to him. It had always been his sanctuary, the place where he could be free from distractions, free from the pressure. Maybe if he went there, he would find some clarity.

The hills stood in the distance, their silhouette outlined against the pale blue sky. He had run up those hills countless times, pushing himself to the limit, feeling the burn in his legs, the strain in his chest, always striving to be faster, to be the best. But today, as he walked toward them, he felt a quiet resistance within himself, as if his body was telling him to stop—to pause and reflect before continuing down the same path.

As he reached the foot of the hills, Motagba paused, taking in the view before him. The familiar landscape stretched out before him: the rolling fields, the scattered huts, the village in the distance. It was all so beautiful, so simple. And yet, there was a restlessness within him that couldn't be ignored.

He sat down on a large rock, the cool surface grounding him as he stared at the horizon. His mind drifted back to the race—the way his heart had pounded in his chest, the way everything had felt so intense in that moment, only to fade away afterward, leaving him with this hollow sense of having accomplished something that didn't fulfill him.

"What am I running for?" he whispered to himself, the question lingering in the air like the morning mist.

The wind rustled the leaves around him, as if the earth itself were listening. He closed his eyes, trying to calm his racing thoughts. His father's voice echoed in his mind, a voice full of wisdom and strength, but it also carried the weight of expectations. His family had always looked to him to be the one who would carry their legacy forward, the one who would continue the tradition of speed that had been passed down through generations. But Motagba didn't know if he could carry that burden anymore.

He thought of Ireti. The way she had looked at him after the race. There had been no jealousy in her eyes, no anger. Instead, there had been understanding—a quiet recognition that the race was not the end. They both knew that. But there was something else, something that felt unresolved between them. They had shared a bond, a friendship forged through the challenges of training together, but now, that bond felt fragile, as if it could break at any moment.

Motagba opened his eyes, his gaze falling to the ground in front of him. His reflection stared back at him in the small pool of water formed by the morning dew. For a moment, he didn't recognize the face staring back at him. The boy he saw there was familiar, but somehow different. His eyes were tired, his face etched with a kind of weariness that didn't match the youthful energy he had once felt. How had he become so distant from himself?

He reached into his pocket and pulled out a small stone, one he had found while running in the hills years ago. It was smooth, worn down by time, and he had kept it with him ever since. A small token, a reminder of the simple joys he had once found in running—before it all became about winning, about expectations. He held the stone in his palm, feeling its weight.

The sound of footsteps broke his reverie, and he looked up to see Ireti walking toward him. Her expression was softer than before, though there was still a hint of something unspoken between them. She stopped a few feet away, her hands resting on her hips as she surveyed the landscape.

"Mind if I join you?" she asked, her voice calm and steady.

Motagba didn't answer right away. Instead, he simply nodded, moving over slightly to make space for her. She sat down beside him, her presence a quiet comfort. The two of them sat in silence for a few moments, the only sound the wind rustling through the trees and the distant calls of birds. It wasn't an uncomfortable silence, but one filled with a kind of understanding—an understanding that there were things neither of them knew how to express yet.

"You've been quiet lately," Ireti said finally, her voice gentle but probing. "I can tell something's been on your mind since the race. You've won, Motagba. What's bothering you?"

Motagba sighed, running his fingers over the smooth stone in his hand. "I don't know. It's just... it doesn't feel the way I thought it would. The race, the victory—it was supposed to mean something more. But now that it's over, I don't feel any different. I thought it would fill some kind of void inside me, but it's like it just opened up more questions instead."

Ireti looked at him, her gaze thoughtful. "You know, I thought the same thing. I thought winning would give me all the answers, that it would prove something to myself, to everyone else. But sometimes, the harder we chase after something, the more it slips away. Maybe it's not the race that matters, but the reason we run in the first place."

Motagba glanced at her, surprised by the depth of her words. "The reason we run?"

She nodded. "Yeah. The reason we do anything. Maybe it's not about winning, or proving something to our families or the village. Maybe it's about finding out who we really are along the way. What if we're running to discover ourselves, not just to get to the finish line?"

Motagba stared at her, the weight of her words settling over him. Could it be that simple? Could it really be about something other than victory, something more profound?

For the first time in a long time, Motagba felt a small flicker of something inside him—hope, maybe, or clarity. It wasn't much, but it was a start. He wasn't sure where the path ahead would lead him, but he knew one thing: it wasn't about the race anymore. It was about the journey, the questions, and the answers he would discover along the way.

As the sun began to rise higher in the sky, Motagba stood up, feeling the warmth of the light on his skin. He didn't have all the answers yet, but for the first time, he felt like he was on the right path. And that, in itself, was enough.

"Thanks, Ireti," he said, his voice steady. "I think I understand a little more now."

She smiled, a quiet understanding in her eyes. "Anytime, Motagba. We're all running toward something, whether we realize it or not. Just make sure you're running for the right reasons."

And with that, the two of them stood together, watching the day unfold before them, knowing that the race was never truly about the finish line—it was about the journey, the questions, and the discoveries that lay ahead.

4

The Crossroads of the Heart

The days following their quiet conversation in the hills were filled with an unfamiliar sense of peace for Motagba. The burden that had weighed heavily on his heart began to lift, slowly but surely. He no longer felt as if he were running toward something undefined, chasing an elusive goal that was forever out of reach. Instead, he found himself taking time to reflect, allowing the answers to unfold gently, in their own time. But as the village continued with its rhythms—its morning songs, its market chatter, the laughter of children playing in the streets—Motagba couldn't shake the feeling that something larger was at play, something beyond his own quest for understanding.

Though his days were quieter now, he knew something was changing within him. Each step he took felt lighter, as if he were beginning to shed layers of himself that no longer served him. But beneath it all, there was still an unanswered question—the question of his future. He had been born into a lineage of runners, into a world where speed was the measure of everything, and winning was the key to honor. But what if running wasn't his destiny? What if the thing that had driven him for so long no longer held the answers?

It was at dusk, on a warm evening that smelled of earth and rain, that Motagba found himself standing at the edge of the village, staring out at the long road that led to the neighboring towns. The road stretched before him, darkening with the setting sun, and he could almost hear it calling to him. The road had always symbolized the future, the unknown, and he had walked it many times before. But this time, it felt different. The village, with all its memories and history, was behind him, and the road ahead seemed to whisper of new beginnings.

"Where do I go from here?" Motagba whispered to himself, unsure if he was asking the road or his own heart.

The cool breeze tugged at his clothes, and in the distance, he could hear the voices of his family preparing for the evening meal. It was the familiar sound of home, of security. But there was an odd feeling of being torn—torn between the life he had always known and the unknown future that beckoned like a shadow on the horizon.

He had spent so much time running, so much time chasing the next race, that he hadn't truly stopped to think about where he was headed, beyond the finish line. The question now was not about winning—it was about choosing a path, about taking control of his own destiny.

"I can't stay here forever," Motagba said softly, more to himself than anyone else.

"Motagba!"

He turned at the sound of his name, his heart skipping a beat. It was Ireti, her presence as calm and steady as always, but there was a hint of something else in her voice. She walked toward him with purpose, her eyes searching his face for something, as if she could see the thoughts churning behind his eyes.

"I didn't expect to find you here," she said, stopping a few feet away, her gaze lingering on him.

"Here, at the edge of the village?" Motagba asked, offering a faint smile. He hadn't realized how much of his thoughts had been on his own until now, but Ireti's presence always seemed to draw him out of himself, to ground him.

"No," she said, shaking her head. "I meant in this place, at this crossroads."

Motagba frowned, his heart pounding in his chest as he met her gaze. "What do you mean?"

"I can see it in your eyes," Ireti said softly. "There's something different about you lately, something that's changed. You're not the same person who raced at the festival. You're searching for something, Motagba. But it's not the next race or the next victory. It's something deeper."

Motagba looked away, uncertain how to respond. She was right, of course. He had been running, but not in the way she meant. It wasn't the same rush of adrenaline that came with the competition. It was a more internal race, a race to understand himself, to make peace with who he was becoming.

"I don't know what I'm searching for," he confessed, his voice heavy with the weight of his uncertainty. "All I've known is running, and now, I don't know if that's enough anymore. There's so much more I'm beginning to realize, things I've never even considered."

Ireti took a few steps closer, her voice filled with quiet empathy. "That's okay. You don't have to know all the answers right now. Not everything can be figured out in a day, or a week, or even a year. Sometimes, it's about the journey, not the destination."

Motagba felt a weight lift off his chest at her words. It was as if a veil had been lifted from his eyes, and he was finally beginning to see that there was more to life than winning, more to life than running. The world was vast, full of possibilities he had never even considered.

"I've always believed that my destiny was tied to speed," he said quietly, almost as if talking to himself. "That I was meant to run, to race. But now... now I'm not so sure."

Ireti smiled softly, a knowing glint in her eyes. "Maybe your destiny is not just about running. Maybe it's about running toward something—toward something greater. Maybe you're meant to run with purpose, with a heart full of courage, toward a future that's beyond the track, beyond the village. It's about more than just winning."

Motagba's eyes widened, as if her words had struck something deep within him. For the first time in a long time, he felt a sense of possibility open up before him. It was like the road ahead was no longer a place of uncertainty, but a place where he could choose the direction he wanted to go.

"You really think so?" he asked, his voice quiet but hopeful.

"I know so," Ireti said confidently. "Your heart has always been racing toward something, Motagba. Now, it's time to listen to it, to see what it's really telling you. You don't have to have all the answers today, but you can start moving toward them. One step at a time."

Motagba looked at her, his heart swelling with gratitude. She had always been there, standing beside him through all the races, all the victories, all the doubts. And now, she was here again, helping him navigate the unknown, helping him understand that there was more to life than the finish line.

The two of them stood in silence for a moment, the soft breeze moving around them, carrying with it the scent of rain and earth. Motagba's heart still raced, but it wasn't the familiar race of competition. It was the race of discovery, the race of self-realization, the race toward a future that was yet unwritten.

"I think I'm ready to listen," Motagba said finally, his voice steady and strong.

"I'm ready to start running for something different."

Ireti smiled, her eyes shining with pride. "Then let's run together. We don't have to figure it all out right away, but we can take the first step."

And so, with the sun setting behind them and the road ahead stretching into the unknown, Motagba took the first step toward a future full of questions, full of possibilities. He didn't know what lay ahead, but for the first time, he was ready to find out. Together with Ireti, he was no longer running to win. He was running to discover who he was meant to be.

5

The Storm and the Calm

The winds had begun to shift. It started as a mere whisper, the kind of gentle breeze that hinted at something larger brewing in the distance. But Motagba could feel it—a change, like a storm gathering, just beyond the horizon. The village, with its quiet routine and familiar rhythms, had always seemed like a safe haven, a place where everything was predictable. But now, the air was thick with the promise of something different, something that would test not just his body, but his heart, and the very essence of who he was.

Motagba stood at the edge of the village again, looking out at the road that stretched before him, the same road that had once seemed so full of uncertainty. But now, as the first drops of rain began to fall, he saw it differently. The road was no longer a symbol of fear or the unknown—it was a place where answers waited, answers he was ready to find. It was as if his heart had finally caught up with his mind, and together they were ready to face whatever lay ahead.

Behind him, the village was already preparing for the storm. The elders gathered around the fire, speaking in hushed tones about the changes they had seen in the skies. The women hurried to secure their homes, pulling in laundry and checking that windows were closed tightly. The children played under the ever-darkening sky, unaware of the impending storm, their laughter filling the air like music.

But Motagba wasn't worried about the storm that was coming in the form of rain or thunder. It was the storm within him that had been building, the one that had been quietly churning since the day he had decided to seek something greater than the race. It was the storm of self-doubt, of uncertainty, of the deep questions that had risen in his heart.

Was this really the path for him? Could he truly walk away from everything he had known? The world of running, of competitions, had always given him purpose. It was simple, straightforward. He ran. He won. And life moved forward. But now, with every conversation he had, every moment of reflection, he felt the pull of something bigger—a life that wasn't measured by victories on a track, but by the choices he made and the impact he could have on the world.

"Ireti was right," he whispered to himself, his voice barely audible against the growing wind. "I need to listen to my heart. But what if it leads me somewhere I'm not ready for?"

A flash of lightning lit up the sky, followed by the distant rumble of thunder. The storm was coming closer, and Motagba could feel the weight of it, pressing down on him like a heavy cloud. It wasn't just the physical storm, but the emotional and spiritual turmoil that had taken root deep within him.

He turned to walk back to the village, but just as he did, a figure appeared in front of him. It was Ireti, her silhouette standing strong against the gathering storm. She looked calm, as if the winds and rain had no power over her. Her presence was a quiet reassurance in the midst of his turmoil.

"You're not alone in this," she said softly, her voice steady despite the rising winds. "I know it feels like the world is shifting beneath you, but it's only because you're changing, Motagba. And change is never easy. But you can face it. You've always been stronger than you know."

Motagba stopped in his tracks, his heart pounding in his chest. He had never shared the depth of his doubts with Ireti. He had always tried to appear certain, confident even, in front of her. But in this moment, with the storm gathering around him, he couldn't hide from the truth any longer.

"I don't know if I'm ready for all this," he admitted, his voice low. "I've spent so much of my life running. I don't even know who I am without that. Without the races. Without the victories."

Ireti's gaze softened as she took a step closer to him, her eyes reflecting the storm in a way that made him feel understood. "It's okay not to have all the answers, Motagba. The important thing is that you're asking the questions. And sometimes, asking is the first step toward finding your way."

Motagba sighed, his shoulders heavy with the weight of his uncertainty. The storm was no longer a metaphor for his inner turmoil—it had become a tangible presence, something that could no longer be ignored. It was all around him, in the thunder that cracked the sky and the rain that began to fall in sheets, soaking him through.

"I feel like I'm standing on the edge of everything I've ever known," Motagba said quietly, almost to himself. "And I don't know if I can cross it. What if I fail? What if I'm not who I think I am?"

"You will never know unless you take the first step," Ireti said gently, placing a hand on his shoulder. "The storm may seem frightening, but it's through the storms that we grow, Motagba. Through the trials, through the challenges. You're not meant to stay in one place forever."

The rain began to pour, but Motagba barely noticed. His mind was racing with thoughts, and in that moment, it was as if the storm outside and the storm within were one and the same. It was the crossroads. The place where the past and the future met, where he had to choose the direction his life would take.

The world around him seemed to fade into the background as he stood there with Ireti, her steady presence grounding him in a way nothing else could. The winds howled, and the rain lashed at their skin, but all Motagba could hear was the sound of his own heart, racing with uncertainty and possibility.

"I've always been afraid of what I might lose," Motagba said, his voice barely audible above the wind. "Afraid that if I step away from what I know, I'll lose everything that matters."

"You're not losing anything," Ireti said, her voice firm, unwavering. "You're gaining everything. The world is bigger than the path you've always known. It's time for you to see that."

Motagba closed his eyes, his mind still racing. But somewhere in the midst of the storm, he found a flicker of clarity. The storm was not just a challenge—it was an opportunity. An opportunity to break free from the limits he had set for himself, to find his true path, and to embrace whatever future awaited him.

The rain soaked him through, and the winds howled louder, but Motagba stood tall, feeling a strange sense of calm settle over him. The storm outside was fierce, but inside, he had found something stronger—a resolve. He wasn't sure where the road ahead would lead, or what trials he would face, but he was ready to face them. Ready to step beyond the finish line of his past and into the unknown.

"I'm ready," Motagba said quietly, his voice steady despite the storm that raged around him.

Ireti smiled, her face illuminated by the flashes of lightning. "Then let's walk forward together. The storm will pass, but what you learn from it will stay with you forever."

With that, they turned toward the village, their steps in sync, moving through the rain, through the storm, together. Motagba knew that the road ahead would not be easy, but for the first time, he felt certain of one thing—he was no longer running from the storm. He was running toward it. And in that, he would find his strength.

6

The Unseen Path

The next morning, the storm had passed, leaving in its wake a sky washed clean and bright, with the earth beneath it still heavy with the promise of renewal. Motagba stood at the edge of the village once again, looking out at the horizon where the sun was beginning to rise, painting the world in hues of gold and orange. The air was cool, and the scent of rain lingered, mingling with the earthy aroma of the land. It felt like the world was waking up anew, and for the first time in days, Motagba felt a sense of peace.

But peace was fleeting. In the silence that followed the storm, the questions that had been swirling in his heart began to resurface, louder than ever. Was he truly ready to leave behind everything he had known? Could he really step away from the races, the victories, and the glory that had defined him for so long?

As much as he wanted to believe he was ready for something new, a deep-rooted fear still clung to him like a shadow. What if he failed? What if the path ahead wasn't as clear as he imagined it? The thought made his chest tighten, his breath quicken. But then, he remembered Ireti's words: *"The storm may seem frightening, but it's through the storms that we grow."*

Perhaps this was his storm. Perhaps the fear he felt now was just another challenge to overcome, another step toward the man he was becoming.

Motagba turned away from the horizon and walked back into the village. The sun was high now, casting long shadows on the dirt roads and illuminating the vibrant colors of the people going about their morning chores. The women gathered at the well, the children played near the marketplace, and the men worked together to mend fences and prepare for the day's tasks.

It was as if nothing had changed. And yet, everything had. The village that had once seemed so familiar now felt different, distant somehow. It was as if he was seeing it for the first time—like he was standing on the edge of his past and his future, unsure of which direction to take.

As he walked through the village, he saw a group of the younger runners gathered by the training grounds, their eyes locked on him. They greeted him with respectful nods, but there was a question in their eyes—one he didn't want to face.

"You've been quiet lately," one of the boys, Niran, said as Motagba approached. "Everything alright?"

Motagba smiled softly, though it didn't reach his eyes. "Just thinking," he replied, his voice distant. "You know how it is."

Niran raised an eyebrow. "Yeah, I guess I do. But you're Motagba, right? You're always so sure, so focused. Everyone looks up to you. So… what's going on?"

The words hit Motagba like a blow to the chest. He had always prided himself on being a pillar of strength, the one people could turn to for answers. But now, with the storm inside him still raging, he wasn't sure if he could offer anyone anything.

"I'm just trying to figure out what's next," Motagba said quietly, his gaze drifting toward the training track in the distance. "You know, sometimes we get so caught up in what's in front of us, that we forget to look at the bigger picture."

Niran nodded, though he didn't seem to fully understand. But there was something in Motagba's voice—something raw and vulnerable—that made the boy fall silent.

"I'll figure it out," Motagba added, forcing a smile. "But for now, you all keep training. There's still a race to be won, and I won't be the one to hold you back."

As the group dispersed, Motagba stood there, watching them with a mixture of pride and sorrow. He had spent so many years teaching them, guiding them, helping them grow. But now, as they raced ahead, he felt like he was falling behind. The thought weighed on him, heavy and persistent.

He turned and walked toward the small hut at the edge of the village, where Ireti often spent her days. She had become a constant presence in his life, a source of comfort and wisdom in the midst of his uncertainty. He had never expected to find someone who understood him so completely, but she had become the steady hand that had guided him through the storm, even when he wasn't sure where he was headed.

When he arrived at the hut, Ireti was sitting outside, a basket of fruits beside her. Her eyes were closed, and she looked peaceful, as if the world's troubles couldn't touch her. But when she heard his footsteps, she opened her eyes and smiled.

"You look like you've been carrying the weight of the world on your shoulders," she said softly, as Motagba sat down beside her.

"I feel like I am," Motagba replied, his voice heavy with emotion. "I don't know what I'm supposed to do anymore, Ireti. I'm not sure if I should keep running or if there's something else I'm meant to do."

Ireti's gaze softened as she placed a hand on his. "You've always known what you wanted, Motagba. But sometimes, knowing the next step isn't as clear as we hope. Sometimes, we have to walk in the dark before the light appears."

Motagba sighed, looking out at the landscape. "I don't know if I'm ready to walk in the dark. What if I stumble? What if I fall?"

"You won't fall," Ireti said confidently. "You've been preparing for this moment your whole life. The races, the victories, they were just the beginning. What's coming next is bigger than anything you've ever done. You just have to trust yourself. Trust that you are enough, even when you can't see the end."

Motagba closed his eyes, taking a deep breath. He didn't have all the answers, and maybe he never would. But in that moment, with Ireti's words ringing in his ears, he felt something shift within him—a quiet resolve, a recognition that the path ahead, though unclear, was his to walk.

"I'll try," he said quietly, the weight on his shoulders lifting just a little. "I'll try to trust myself."

Ireti smiled. "That's all you can do. The rest will come when you're ready."

As the sun climbed higher in the sky, the village continued its rhythm, its pulse steady and unwavering. But for Motagba, the rhythm of his life had changed. The track no longer called to him with the same intensity, the races no longer held the same allure. The world beyond the village, beyond the finish line, had become more important. And in that, he had found a new purpose.

The unseen path before him was uncertain, but it was his to discover. And for the first time in a long while, Motagba was ready to take the first step.

7

The First Step

The early morning mist hung low over the village, swirling around the familiar shapes of houses and the distant trees. The air was thick with the scent of damp earth and dew, carrying with it a cool freshness that seemed to settle deep within Motagba's bones. He stood at the entrance of the village, looking out at the long, winding path that led into the heart of the wilderness. The path was not new, but today it felt different—like a door that had been waiting to be opened, waiting for him to step through.

Behind him, the village was still waking up, the sounds of roosters crowing, children laughing, and women chattering at the market just beginning to rise. But Motagba, though part of this world, felt a disconnection. Something had shifted in him. He could no longer be content with the familiar. He needed more. He needed to know what lay beyond, what other parts of the world had to offer.

He turned away from the path for a moment and glanced back at the village. The sight of his home, the place that had shaped him, felt bittersweet. He had spent years running, pushing himself beyond limits to win races and be the best. But now, there was a new race—a race toward a future unknown, one that didn't involve finishing first, but living fully.

THE FIRST STEP

The decision had been made. He couldn't ignore it any longer. The storm inside him had calmed, and now it was time for him to leave the tracks behind, at least for now. The village might always remain in his heart, but it was the world beyond that he had to discover.

With a deep breath, Motagba set his sights on the path again. The heavy steps that had once felt so daunting now seemed like the only way forward. He was ready to take that first step, even if he couldn't see the end of the journey.

"Ireti was right," Motagba muttered to himself. "I have to trust myself."

His mind flashed back to the conversations they'd had in the past weeks. Ireti had always been the voice of reason when he was consumed with doubt. She had reminded him time and time again that growth came from discomfort. He was leaving the world of certainty, but it was in the unknown that he would find new strengths, new purpose.

He hadn't shared his decision with many, only a few close friends. He wasn't sure if they would understand, but he knew it was something he had to do. His family, too, would likely wonder why he was stepping away from the world of racing, from the fame and recognition that had come with it. They'd raised him with the belief that victory and success were the highest honors a person could attain, but he had come to realize that true success didn't always look the way others expected it to.

Motagba paused before he left the village gates, looking back one last time. The small, familiar details—the sun rising over the hill, the old man sweeping the dirt road, the scent of breakfast cooking from the nearby homes—felt like pieces of his past that he would carry with him. There was a comfort in these things, a safety that had cradled him for so long. But there was also a restlessness, a pull toward something more.

He didn't know what awaited him. He didn't know if he was prepared for the challenges ahead. But what he did know was that he was no longer afraid of the uncertainty. He had embraced it.

As he took that first step toward the open road, a quiet confidence settled over him. The path wasn't clear, and the way forward was not easy. But every journey, no matter how difficult, begins with a single step. And Motagba was taking it, with his heart racing, but this time, not from fear—this time, it was from anticipation.

The road ahead was long and uncertain, but he was ready to walk it. There was much to learn, much to see, and much to experience. And though he was leaving behind the only life he had known, Motagba felt a strange sense of peace. He was finally becoming the man he had always wanted to be—the man who was not defined by his past, but by the choices he made in the present, and the courage he showed in the face of the unknown.

As he walked into the wilderness, the sun rising higher in the sky, Motagba knew he was no longer racing to be the fastest. He was racing toward something much more important—toward the fullness of life, toward growth, and toward finding the courage to embrace change.

With each step, the village faded behind him, but the future was slowly taking shape. The journey was just beginning.

8

The Unknown Horizon

Days passed since Motagba had left the village. The landscape around him gradually shifted from the familiar, rolling hills of his homeland to the dense, untamed wilderness that lay ahead. Each step he took seemed to carry him farther from the village, farther from everything he had ever known. The initial excitement of his decision had been replaced by a quiet contemplation, a deep awareness of just how vast the world was and how little he truly understood about it.

The road before him was often difficult to follow. The path was overgrown in places, twisted by the changing seasons, and at times, he found himself cutting through dense brush or climbing over rocks that seemed determined to slow his progress. There were moments when he questioned his decision—when the weight of uncertainty pressed down on him so heavily that it almost felt as if the earth itself was trying to swallow him whole.

But then, in the silence of the wilderness, Motagba would remember his purpose. It was the thought of growth, of self-discovery, that had driven him to take this step in the first place. He was no longer the young man who had defined himself by his ability to run fast or win races. The man walking this path was someone who was seeking something deeper—something that could not be measured by time, distance, or victory.

It wasn't long before he came across his first real challenge on the journey. As he trekked through a particularly dense part of the forest, the air growing thick with the scent of wet foliage, he suddenly heard the unmistakable sound of rushing water. His pace quickened as he followed the sound, hoping to find a river or a stream to refresh himself.

But as he neared the source of the noise, he discovered something far more daunting: a wide, fast-flowing river, its waters swollen by the recent rains. The current was strong, and the river stretched as far as the eye could see in both directions. There was no bridge in sight, and the water churned violently, making it impossible to cross by foot.

Motagba stopped at the edge of the river, staring at the powerful flow with a mixture of awe and uncertainty. This was not something he had expected to encounter on his journey. The river represented a physical barrier, something that stood between him and the next step of his path. For a moment, he wondered if this was the end of the road for him. How could he possibly continue if the river blocked his way?

But then, as he stood there, watching the water rush past him, a memory surfaced—one of his father's teachings, a lesson he had heard countless times as a child.

"Every obstacle is a test, Motagba," his father's voice echoed in his mind. "The path to greatness is never straight. It is filled with challenges that force us to become stronger, to think differently, to find a way through."

Motagba's heart quickened, not from fear, but from recognition. This was the very thing his father had meant. The obstacle in front of him was not a reason to turn back; it was an opportunity to learn, to adapt, and to grow.

He stood at the river's edge for a long while, considering his options. There was no bridge, and crossing directly seemed too dangerous. But there were trees nearby, their thick trunks reaching high into the air, with strong branches that could potentially offer a way across. Motagba studied them carefully, eyeing the trees with a sense of purpose.

With determination in his step, he began to work. He first found a sturdy vine that hung from one of the trees. Testing it with his hands, he confirmed that it was strong enough to support his weight. Slowly, he climbed the tree, using the vine as support to hoist himself higher. The climb was difficult—his muscles strained as he pulled himself up—but he refused to let the river's challenge defeat him. This was part of the journey.

Once he reached a high enough branch, Motagba found a sturdy section of wood to balance himself on, carefully inching his way across the tree to the next, closer branch. He used every ounce of his training, both physical and mental, to stay focused on the task at hand. His heart raced with both excitement and fear, but he kept moving forward, one careful step at a time.

After what seemed like hours, but in truth was only a matter of minutes, Motagba finally reached the other side. His feet touched solid ground once again, and he took a moment to steady himself, breathing deeply and allowing the thrill of success to settle into his bones. He had done it. The obstacle had been overcome, not by rushing or avoiding it, but by patiently finding a way through.

He looked back at the river, its waters still rushing beneath the trees. There was no sign of the fear he had felt moments before. Instead, a feeling of triumph washed over him. He had crossed the river, not just physically, but mentally. The journey was never going to be easy, but with every obstacle, he would grow stronger. This was just the beginning.

Motagba continued walking, the path ahead still unknown, but the weight of uncertainty seemed lighter now. Every step he took seemed to be filled with purpose, each moment a piece of the puzzle that would eventually come together in ways he couldn't yet see.

As he walked deeper into the wilderness, he felt a change taking place within himself. The world around him, so vast and intimidating at first, was beginning to feel more like home. The trees, the rivers, the distant mountains—they were all part of the same journey he had started. And though the path was still unclear, he had learned something crucial on this day. The fear of the unknown was always going to be there, but the courage to face it was what mattered most.

He had faced the river. And now, with his heart racing with the thrill of accomplishment, he knew that there would be no obstacle that could stop him from continuing the journey.

As the sun began to set, casting long shadows across the land, Motagba felt a sense of peace settle over him. There was no turning back now. The unknown horizon was no longer a source of fear, but a place of possibility. And he was ready to walk toward it, one step at a time.

9

The Silent Mentor

Days blurred into one another as Motagba continued his journey through the wild. The landscape seemed to stretch endlessly before him, shifting from dense forest to open plains, from hills to deep valleys, and back again. Every day was an adventure, each step carrying him further into the unknown. Yet, despite the beauty and awe that the world around him inspired, a part of him still struggled with the loneliness that came with traveling alone.

Though he had left behind the familiar faces of his village, there were times when he longed for the comfort of companionship. It was during these moments of quiet reflection that he remembered the conversations he had shared with his old mentor, Baba Akintoye, back in the village. Baba Akintoye had been an elderly man who had spent much of his life teaching the young ones about the deeper meanings of existence, about balance, about understanding the rhythm of life.

In the past, Motagba had taken Baba Akintoye's lessons lightly, assuming that the wisdom passed down by the older generations was merely a collection of stories and morals. Now, as he walked this lonely road, Motagba found himself thinking more and more about the old man's words.

"Sometimes, the greatest lessons are not spoken," Baba Akintoye had said one evening as they sat together on the steps of the village council hall. "True understanding comes from listening to the silence. Life does not speak in words, but in moments, in the quiet spaces between your thoughts. That's where you'll find your answers."

Motagba had never truly understood what Baba Akintoye meant by this, but now, as he journeyed deeper into the wilderness, the meaning of the old man's words began to take shape.

It was the third morning after his crossing of the river, and the air had taken on a crisp chill as the sun rose slowly over the horizon. Motagba had been walking for hours, his muscles sore from the day before, when he came across a small clearing. It wasn't much, just a patch of dry earth surrounded by dense trees, but there was something about it that felt different. It felt... inviting.

He paused and sat down on a large stone, taking a moment to rest. The exhaustion from the journey weighed on him, but it was the quiet that truly struck him in that moment. It was as though the world itself had fallen into stillness—no birds singing, no wind rustling the leaves, no animals moving through the underbrush. It was a profound silence that enveloped everything.

Motagba closed his eyes and took a deep breath. His thoughts, as they had so often done on this journey, began to race. He wondered where he was headed, what his purpose was. The challenges he had faced so far had been difficult, but nothing compared to the uncertainty that lay ahead. He had no map, no guide, only his instincts to lead him.

Then, as though on cue, the stillness around him seemed to shift. Motagba's heart beat a little faster as he felt a subtle presence, not of someone physically near him, but of something—something that had always been there but had remained hidden until now.

He opened his eyes and looked around. The clearing was unchanged. Yet, the feeling that he was not alone lingered. Slowly, he stood up, his feet moving without much thought as he walked toward the center of the clearing. His instincts were guiding him, nudging him forward as if urging him to listen.

And then, he saw it—an old tree, unlike any other in the surrounding forest. Its bark was cracked and weathered, its branches gnarled and twisted, but there was something undeniably ancient about it, as though it had witnessed the passage of time in ways no human could comprehend. It was the kind of tree that could have easily been overlooked, blending into the wilderness, but Motagba felt drawn to it.

He stood before it, the weight of his decision to leave his village suddenly pressing on him again. What had he really hoped to find out here in the wilderness? Was this journey about more than just escaping the confines of the village? Was it about understanding who he truly was, beyond the title of the fastest runner?

Motagba reached out and placed a hand gently on the tree's rough bark. The sensation that passed through him was unlike anything he had ever felt before—neither pain nor pleasure, but a strange kind of understanding, as if the tree was sharing something with him. The air around him seemed to hum with quiet energy, and the world felt at once both distant and intimately close.

As he stood there, his mind began to quiet. The racing thoughts slowed, and the questions that had plagued him for so long faded into the background. In that moment, he realized that the journey he was on was not just about finding answers—it was about embracing the silence, the spaces between the words, and trusting that they held the wisdom he sought.

For a long while, Motagba remained there, standing in silence before the tree, feeling a connection that transcended words. There was no profound revelation, no grand moment of clarity. There was only the peace of being in the present, of being one with the world around him.

It was in that quiet, unspoken moment that Motagba realized something crucial. The journey he had embarked upon was not about overcoming obstacles, nor was it about reaching a destination. It was about becoming attuned to the flow of life, about learning to listen—to the world, to the silence, and to himself.

The tree had not spoken, nor had any voice appeared to guide him. But in the stillness, he had found something far more valuable: a sense of connection, a deeper understanding of his place in the world. He didn't need to know the future. He didn't need to know where the road would lead. What mattered now was that he was walking it, fully present, and ready to embrace whatever came next.

Motagba finally pulled his hand away from the tree and took a deep breath. The silence lingered, but it no longer felt empty. Instead, it felt full—full of potential, full of promise. He had learned, in his own way, to listen.

As he turned to leave the clearing, he looked back at the ancient tree one last time. Though the world had not changed, and his journey was far from over, Motagba felt something shift inside him. He was no longer running away from something. He was running toward something—toward the deeper understanding of himself, toward the wisdom of silence, and toward the unknown horizon that beckoned him forward.

And so, with a heart steady and strong, he continued his journey.

10

The Return of the Heart

The days following Motagba's experience in the silent clearing passed with an ease that surprised him. Though the path remained rugged, and the wilderness still held its many challenges, there was a calm within him that had not existed before. The journey had become more than a search for answers—it had become a pilgrimage of the heart. Each step was no longer just a movement through the forest or across hills; it was a step toward understanding, a step toward growth.

Motagba had learned to find peace in the silence of the world around him. He had learned that answers did not always come in the form of words, nor did they arrive in an instant. Sometimes, they came slowly, like the steady drip of rain on a dry earth. In the time he had spent walking through the wilderness, Motagba had come to understand that his life was not meant to be a race toward a specific destination. It was a journey—one that required patience, trust, and acceptance.

But as he moved forward, he felt a shift in the air, a subtle tug within him that reminded him of the life he had left behind. The thought of home, of the village where his family lived, began to stir in him a deep longing. For all the lessons he had learned out here, there was still something important waiting for him in that distant place.

One evening, as the sky turned a brilliant orange, Motagba stopped at a high point in the landscape, overlooking the valley where his village lay. The setting sun cast a warm glow over the land, and for the first time since leaving, he could see the place where his journey had begun. It felt as though the village was calling to him, beckoning him back with the promise of something new—something beyond the races he had once run or the expectations others had of him.

He stood there for a long while, just watching, feeling a pull in his heart that he could not ignore. The wilderness had given him many gifts—insight, strength, clarity—but it had also given him a sense of direction. And that direction was now leading him home.

The decision to return was not a difficult one. Motagba knew that his time in the wilderness had been necessary. He had needed to be away from the familiar, to face the unknown, and to come to terms with who he was beyond the title of the fastest runner. But he also understood that life, much like a race, was about balance. It was about knowing when to push forward and when to return to what you know, to what grounds you. His heart had grown during his time away, but now it was time to bring that growth back to the village, to share what he had learned, and to offer it to the people who had shaped him.

The path back home was different. What had once seemed long and uncertain now appeared familiar, even welcoming. The dense forests, the streams, the rocky hills—all of them held memories of the journey he had undertaken. But this time, Motagba walked with a newfound understanding. He had seen what lay beyond the village, and now he was returning to it, not as the boy who had once fled for the thrill of the race, but as a man who had learned to embrace both the quiet and the noise, the challenges and the rewards.

As he made his way back, Motagba could feel the weight of the village's expectations on his shoulders. The people there had always expected greatness from him, and he knew they would be eager to see what he had achieved in his time away. But he was no longer the person they had known. He was not just the fastest runner; he was someone who had learned to listen, to reflect, and to grow in ways they might not yet understand. He was no longer a man defined by his speed; he was a man who had found his purpose, a man who had come to know the true meaning of strength.

When he finally entered the village, it was late in the afternoon. The streets were quiet, and the usual hum of activity was absent. As he walked down the familiar paths, his heart beat faster, a mix of anticipation and nervousness coursing through him. He had imagined this moment many times on his journey, but now that it had arrived, he felt the weight of its significance. He was returning not just as a traveler, but as someone who had been changed by what he had experienced.

He passed by the familiar homes, the ones where he had spent his childhood, and he noticed the familiar faces peeking out from behind doors and windows. The village had not changed much in his absence. It was still the same place, with the same people, and yet, Motagba felt as though he was seeing it through new eyes. The simplicity of village life, once so confining, now seemed rich with meaning. The everyday rituals, the conversations, the laughter—it was all part of the fabric of life that he had once taken for granted.

As he reached his family's home, Motagba was greeted by his mother, who had been standing outside, waiting for his return. Her eyes lit up when she saw him, and she ran to embrace him, tears welling in her eyes. "My son," she said, her voice filled with both relief and joy. "You are back."

Motagba held her close, the love and warmth of his mother enveloping him in a way that no wilderness or distant journey could ever replicate. It was then that he realized the true depth of the lessons he had learned. The journey had been important, but it was the people he had left behind that truly mattered. The village, his family, his community—these were the things that grounded him, that gave his life meaning.

"I've missed you, mother," Motagba said softly, his voice thick with emotion. "I've missed home."

She smiled, pulling back to look at him, her eyes searching his face for signs of change. "You have been gone so long. I wonder what you've learned. What has the world taught you, my son?"

Motagba paused, his gaze drifting over the village before him. "I have learned many things, mother," he said, his voice steady but filled with conviction. "I have learned that life is not just about running fast or winning races. It is about understanding who we are, what we stand for, and where we belong. It is about the moments of silence and the times of challenge. And it is about knowing when to return, when to go back to where it all began, to share what you've learned with the people who helped shape you."

His mother nodded, her expression filled with pride. "You have learned well, my son. And I am proud of you."

That night, the village gathered to welcome Motagba back. The elders, the youth, and the children all gathered in the village square, eager to hear about his journey. But as Motagba stood before them, he did not speak of his triumphs, his challenges, or the wisdom he had gained in the wilderness. Instead, he shared a simple message.

"All of you," he began, "have shaped me into the man I am today. I left seeking something I didn't fully understand, but I have come to realize that everything I was searching for was here all along—in the quiet of the village, in the hearts of the people who love me, and in the life we share together."

He looked out over the crowd, his heart swelling with gratitude. "I may have run many races in the past, but the greatest race is not the one you win. It is the race to understand yourself, to find peace with who you are, and to return home when the time is right."

And so, Motagba returned—not just as the fastest runner the village had ever known, but as a man who had found his heart, his purpose, and his place in the world. The village rejoiced not because he had won races, but because he had returned home with a wisdom that could not be measured in seconds or medals.

Motagba's heart, once racing with the need to prove himself, now beat steadily with the understanding that his true race had always been one of inner peace, connection, and purpose. The world had given him many gifts, but it was the return home that had finally shown him the greatest lesson of all: that the heart's journey is never truly finished—it only continues to grow, expand, and deepen with each step taken toward understanding.

And so, Motagba's heart raced no more, for it had found its rhythm in the village where his journey had begun.

www.ingramcontent.com/pod-product-compliance
Lightning Source LLC
LaVergne TN
LVHW052049070526
838201LV00086B/5142